RETAIL SHOCK THERAPY

RETAIL SHOCK THERAPY

A Prescription For What Ails Your Online Sales

by
Arlene Battishill, Ph.D.
www.arlenebattishill.com

YOUR FREE GIFTS

As a way of saying thanks for your purchase, Arlene has provided three FREE gifts for you to download from her website:

1. A PDF that provides an excerpt of resources from the book that can help you improve your online sales.

2. A video that shows you how your target audience can make or break your online sales when you're advertising.

3. An E-Book entitled "Everything I Know I Learned From A Pencil: How To Master The Art Of Selling". Understanding just one simple thing can make a huge difference in your online sales.

To get your FREE gifts, go to
http://www.arlenebattishill.com/bonuses.

Copyright

PREFACE

One of the greatest joys of bringing a product to market is when someone purchases it. The act of someone buying your product is a validation that your idea was a good one. That joy, however, can turn to panic when the consumer stops buying. Every business goes through this. It becomes a real test of what you're made of because there is so much at risk and if you can't fix the problem, you may feel like you're going to lose your business.

This book examines a number of things that contribute to why your product isn't selling or isn't selling as well anymore. It covers the things you have no control over and the things you do. It provides a road map for you to analyze your business and your products objectively so that you can determine the best way to jump-start your sales. There's no doubt that it's possible to get your sales going again, it just takes a bit of detective work to determine what the problem is and how you need to respond.

It should be noted that no single book can address every possible reason for why a product isn't selling. There are just too many different products and industries to be able to do that. As a result, this book limits the discussion to those businesses that are selling primarily online. However, even if you're not selling online, this method is still relevant to your product, especially when we get into talking about how to present your product to the consumer in a way that will increase sales.

Finally, for anyone who is thinking of starting a business and launching a product, the things covered in this book are absolutely relevant to you. You can avoid a lot of problems if you take certain actions at the start.

So, with that, let's get started...

THE ELEPHANT IN
THE ROOM

The first thing we have to address is something most people don't want to acknowledge. It goes something like this: you had an idea for a product or a business. You told your friends and family members about your idea and they all told you it was a great idea and you should do it. You spent a whole bunch of time and money creating that product or business without bothering to fully investigate whether the product or business was viable. You were so in love with your idea that you lost your mind and just set about implementing your idea. You didn't do any market research to determine demand. You didn't do any competitive research to determine how many players were in your selling space. You didn't do any pricing research to determine what your profitability might look like. You didn't do any cost analysis to determine if your product could be made in a way that would allow you to operate your business and make a profit. You only had enough money to get your business started but completely forgot about how much it was going to cost you to market and advertise your business. You forgot about this because you never put a budget together that detailed all of the costs you were going to incur as a result of creating your business. You thought that all you had to do was open a store, get a website and a Facebook page and somehow the customers would appear. You then spent an inordinate amount of time and money creating your product and business and then you were open for business. Maybe the customers showed up, maybe they didn't. What is true in this case is that many more customers could have shown up and didn't and you could never figure out why.

I KNOW this isn't you, right?

Well, the problem is, "magical thinking", something most entrepreneurs suffer from. They think if they build it, "they will come". Unfortunately, that only happens in the movies unless, of course, you have some ridiculously fabulous product that solves the world's problems or is something everyone in the world just HAS to have! That isn't most people and it isn't most products.

If any of this is familiar to you, don't worry I get it. I get it because I did it that way myself and have a nearly half million-dollar hole in my bank account to show for it! If this is you, it's okay, it's not the end of the world (unless you ran out of money) and there are things you can do going forward that can make a huge difference in your sales. You're just going to have to do some remedial work to get yourself back on track again.

FIRST, DON'T PANIC!

The first thing you have to recognize when the sales of your product start losing momentum is that there is usually a reason for it. Yes, I know that's rather obvious, right? Well, I bring this up because of what usually happens to an entrepreneur as a result: panic sets in. If you panic, it's going to result in you making really bad decisions. That will only serve to get you further away from what you're trying to do and that is, get your sales back on track.

Another natural tendency when sales of a product are in decline is to start looking at ways to cut costs in your business. This is another huge mistake. Your costs are your costs and those costs don't have anything to do with what's happening with the sales of your product. If you start whacking away at your expenses, you're potentially going to cut yourself off at the knees and really screw up your business. That is NOT what you want to be doing, especially at a time like this!

So, what I'm going to suggest you first is: pour yourself a stiff drink, settle into a comfortable chair and sit back and relax and read the rest of this book! (Note: drinks can be omitted if they prevent you from paying attention!)

THERE'S GOT TO BE
A REASON

One of the things that's really hard for an entrepreneur to accept is that, after all the hard work, money, time, blood, sweat and tears, a product will eventually get to a point where it won't sell anymore. This is what is commonly known as a "Product Life Cycle". I know what you're thinking: who cares about that, all you want to know is what to do about your declining sales. (You can jump to the end of the book to see my checklist for that but none of it will make any sense if you don't read the whole book!) BUT, if you take a moment to understand the reality of what happens over time, it makes it a little easier to be objective about what's happening with your product and then you can be a little less emotional when deciding on what action you need to take.

So, let's take a look at this. In the beginning, back when you developed your product (and probably spent your life savings on it), you spent a ton of money bringing the product to market. Then, you spent ten times more marketing your product so that you finally got to the point where the product was selling and the sales were looking good. The time that this took and the amount of money you spent during this time was largely influenced by how much competition was in the market and your ability to make the consumer aware that you were out there. You may not know that this was the case, but that's how it works.

Once you got to the point where the products were selling, you started making some money. Then maybe, you were able to get your costs of manufacturing down, negotiate better deals with your suppliers (because you had a steady flow of orders), so that everything was pretty good or in some cases, very good. During that time, there was some "jockeying for position" by you and your competition. The good days and the bad days were largely a result of whatever marketing efforts were undertaken by you and the enemy. This little battle continued on a regular basis. You'd have your wins and they'd have theirs. And then, seemingly out of nowhere, your sales either started declining or just dropped off a cliff.

THINGS YOU CAN'T CONTROL

Now that you've had that stiff drink, let's take a look at why this might have happened. Without a doubt, we have to look at whether something has happened with the economy. You probably remember what happened in the mid 2000's when the economy pretty much imploded. Most businesses were left with products they couldn't sell, even at a deep discount. Consumers sucked in their belts to the point where they couldn't breathe and no one was buying anymore. Granted, this is a pretty extreme case and something that doesn't happen very often, but when it does (and it did), rest assured, that shit storm is going to hit everyone (and did), so we're all going down together. Small comfort, I know, but at least we can all wave at each other in our respective lifeboats!

The fact is, when the economy takes a dive, there's pretty much nothing you can do but hang on for dear life and hope that the storm doesn't last too long. Once you've gone through something like this, you'll find yourself making very different decisions about your business. For example, you might be adjusting your inventory levels so that you can minimize the amount of cash you have tied up in inventory. You might limit the selection of products available to the consumer so that you're not holding a bunch of inventory you later won't be able to sell. You might run your business with a skeleton crew just to ensure that you can keep operating through the downturn without having to layoff any of your valued employees. And, you might have to take less money from the business in order to keep it running.

If you believe you have a product that makes sense for the market, meaning there's been a demand for it in the past and you firmly believe that you will come out the other side of a downturn, it's worth it to reduce what you're taking out of the business (in the form of salary or loan repayments to yourself). This should allow you to ride out the storm until a time when you can start paying yourself again.

Another thing you can't control is whether some behemoth company (or even a small one) decides to enter the market with some bright, shiny, new object that steals the eyeballs of your customers and prospects, leaving you feeling like last night's leftovers. It's unknown if Mr. Bright and Shiny is going to be around for a long time, but all you know right now is he's the King of the Block and you have to weather the storm until the shine rubs off or another bright and shiny object steals his thunder (and yours). Like with the economy, this can be temporary but temporary can feel like a lifetime AND have the effect of draining your bank account in the meantime.

Another thing that might be happening is that there is now a preponderance of similar products on the market.

You were the "flavor of the month" for several years but now other products have come on the market like they always do and it's a possibility that the other products are striking a chord with the consumer in a way that your product no longer does.

There is always the risk that the consumer will lose interest in your product, but you have to look at whether they've lost interest because your product is no longer interesting OR because one or more of your competitors is presenting the product to the consumer in a way that is much more compelling. If it's the latter, then there IS something you can do about it. I will talk more about this later.

Now that we've established what you have no control over, let's look at look at some things that you do have control over that might be affecting your online sales. Then we'll look at what you can do about it.

I'M SO BEAUTIFUL, WHY DON'T YOU WANT ME?

There are two overriding issues we need to look at when examining why your products aren't selling: (1) is the issue associated with just one of your products or is it everything you're selling and (2) is the issue associated with visibility or conversions.

The first issue is fairly straightforward and easy to fix because it only involves one of your products. So, we have to start by looking at whether there is anything you can do with that "dog" of a product. How have you presented it to the consumer? Are you using crappy product photos that make the consumer say "No, thanks"? Is the product description unclear or worse, doesn't present the product in a way that makes the consumer want to buy? Does your customer understand the product the second they see it? Is your pricing out of whack?

Let's be clear: you can't afford to fall in love with a product and make bad decisions. It's like the stock market, you invest in something and every market indicator suggests you need to dump the stock and you just keep hanging on because you believe that some miracle is going to happen and the price is going to go up. It's the same way with your product. If you've got a product that isn't selling and you've done everything you can to present the product to the consumer in a way that should be getting them to buy, get rid of it! Mark it down, clear it out and pull your money out.

If you still insist on deluding yourself into thinking you're somehow going to be able to sell that product, do yourself a big favor: ask your customers why they haven't bought it. Your customers will tell you and if you don't want to ask them, post a question on the Reddit.com Entrepreneur page or Quora.com. Ask the general public to give you their thoughts on why the product isn't selling. You already know the rest of your products are selling, but you're hanging on to that one thing. You clearly don't have a visibility problem, you've got a product problem, so get the answer to why people aren't buying it so you can finally let it go and move on.

Now, if the issue you're having is that all of your products aren't selling, we have to get into whether the issue is associated with poor visibility of your products on the Internet or difficulty getting people to buy once they find you.

The issues of visibility and conversion are the major focus of this book. We have to look at why people aren't seeing you as well as, if they are seeing you, why aren't they buying. Most important, we're going to address what you can do to fix both of these things. So, let's take a look at what's going on in your world out on the Internet.

ARE YOUR CUSTOMERS BEATING UP ON YOU?

Let's face it; angry customers lead to angry reviews. We've all had it happen. A customer is unsatisfied with something and blasts you on one of the popular search and review sites like Yelp. They'll post nasty comments on all of your social media accounts and will even take to stalking you on the Internet because they're so pissed off. They might even set up a website and start writing blog posts designed to bash your business. This generally doesn't happen to small businesses but it definitely happens to big ones and you can't afford to let this happen.

When your sales are in decline, you need to be checking all over the Internet to see if there has been any of this negative "speak" in recent weeks or months. This kind of negative "press" can have an immediate and negative impact on your sales and you have to make sure that if it's happening, you deal with it and try and make the situation right with that or those customers. It doesn't matter if they're wrong, the reality is, you cannot afford to have anyone saying anything bad about you on the Internet and if they do, you have to respond to it immediately.

Some of the ways you can "police" what's being said about you on the Internet is to start by setting up a "Google Alert". You can just do a Google search for "Google Alert" and you'll be taken to a link that will show you how to set up these alerts. Put very simply, you enter the name of your business as the keyword you want Google to look for and any time someone enters that word in a Google search, Google will send you an email alerting you to the fact that someone has said something about you on the Internet. It's not always bad news in the alerts. You might find people saying complimentary things about you and that's something you can capitalize on for your business. But, in terms of doing damage control for your business, you need to be constantly monitoring what's being said on the Internet so you can minimize the damage before it's too late.

Another way you can monitor what's being said about you is to check the website buzzsumo.com. This website will provide you with a clickable link to anything that has been said about you on the Internet and will also show you the extent to which that information has been shared across all the major social media platforms (i.e., Facebook, LinkedIn, Twitter, Pinterest, YouTube, etc.). This can be a sobering experience but a necessary one because you can see very quickly whether you've got a customer problem that might be contributing to a decline in your sales.

Also, beware, there is a website called Ripoff Report (www.ripoffreport.com) that allows people to post negative things about your business and there is nothing you can do to make that negative information go away. Ripoff Report has been so successful in getting people to post negative reviews that they have a very high Google search ranking whenever a company has a bad review. As a result, if you have a bad review on that site, it's going to show up near the top of the Google search results when someone is looking for your company. Suffice it to say, you have to control the experience people have with you or it's going to come back to haunt you on the Internet.

ARE YOUR CUSTOMERS ABANDONING YOU?

One of the things you need to look at right away is whether there are sales occurring on your website that aren't being finalized by the customers. These people are hanging out in abandoned shopping carts on your site. If you're not looking at this every day, I can guarantee that you're losing sales you once had.

There are some common reasons people don't complete their purchases. The biggest culprits are that the payment processing on the site got hung up or the website wasn't friendly to people trying to complete a purchase, especially on mobile devices. Other reasons can include finding the product somewhere else they like better, getting a better deal on it somewhere else, finding it on Amazon and getting free shipping or they were really just window shopping. It could also be that they put something in the shopping cart, left the window open on their computer and for some reason, never got back to the open window to complete the purchase.

You can also encounter a big problem if you happen to sell directly to Amazon. If you do, you need to really examine whether it's worth it. While you get the benefit of all of their marketing, you're paying a hefty price for it because of all the fees and incidental costs they charge. You're also paying a price because now all of the Internet traffic for your products is going to Amazon. You can see the sales on your website completely dry up as a result. If people do manage to find your site, it's likely they'll still head over to Amazon to buy because they're getting free shipping. Recognize that even if you offer free shipping on your site, people will still go to Amazon and shop because they might want to include your items with other items they're purchasing on Amazon. As a result, Amazon may not be your friend.

Whatever the reason a customer doesn't complete a purchase and is having their own little private party in your abandoned shopping cart, you have to take immediate action to stem the tide or at least get more information about why they're not completing their purchase.

The best way to deal with this is by making sure your website is set up to generate automatic emails within one hour, twenty-four hours and again in about three days after someone leaves something in their shopping cart. You want to remind the customer that they didn't complete their purchase and then gently nudge them toward completing it. If they don't complete after the first email, the second email needs to offer them something of value, perhaps a 10% discount coupon code. If they still don't buy after the second email, you want to encourage them in the third email to tell you why they didn't complete their purchase. You'd be amazed at the information you can get from people. It could be that you have a credit card processing problem with your site, or something else happened while they were trying to complete their purchase. Whatever you can do to get them to tell you why they didn't complete their purchase is worth money in the bank to you because there's a good chance you can fix the problem and save that sale.

If you don't already know how to set up these emails, here's what you need to do. First, you need to make sure you're using one of the most common e-commerce platforms. These include Magento, WooCommerce, PrestaShop, Shopify, osCommerce, BigCommerce, OpenCart and Volusion to name the most popular. On each of these sites, there will be a menu selection that will pertain to your abandoned shopping cart. It might come in the form of an abandoned cart report. Wherever it's located on your website dashboard, you need to find it so you can check the extent to which people are leaving your site without converting into a buying customer.

You then look for a menu selection on your site (or check the Help section) for the place where you will create your abandoned cart emails. Each system will allow you to create multiple emails that they will send out to the people who didn't complete their purchases. In each email you create, you'll be reminding the customer that they left something in their shopping cart. Your system will automatically insert the information from their shopping cart along with a link back to the shopping cart. The first email is a reminder, the second might offer a discount or another gentle reminder, the third and final will notify them that this is the last email and also ask them for feedback on why they aren't completing their purchase.

The emails will be sent automatically by your e-commerce platform, so for example, this might be within one-hour, 24 hours and three days following the abandonment of a purchase. If you get a response back from the customer, this is a perfect opportunity to evaluate that customer based on what they've shared with you and decide what you want to offer them to get them to complete their purchase. It's also helpful to have this information because it clues you in to reasons why other people might not be completing their purchases. If it's something you can fix right away, you need to do it.

Now, if you have never had these automatic emails set up in your system, you need to do the following. Get your system set up so that for any future shoppers who abandon their cart, the emails will be triggered. Then, go into your abandoned cart report and copy every email address of anyone who has ever attempted to place an order and didn't complete it. You then go over to your email provider such as MailChimp, Constant Contact, aWeber or any of the many other contact management systems ("CMS") and create a new email list. You paste the email addresses into this new list. Then, you create a new email that will be sent to all of these people that will say something like "In a land far away, in a time they forgot, they once tried to purchase on your site and their shopping cart is feeling lonely, just waiting for them to return and collect their items."

Even if these abandon cart people have been gone for months, they are still considered viable sales leads. As such, it's critical to reengage them. It's possible they just might end up completing their orders.

IS YOUR WEBSITE KILLING YOUR SALES?

Crappy selling produces crappy results. In any business, be it your own or one you've worked for, salespeople are the engine of the business. If the salespeople aren't getting the job done, you have no sales, plain and simple. The same thing applies when you're selling online. If your sales "machine" isn't getting the job done, you have no sales and aren't likely to stay in business for very long.

Your sales machine online starts with your website. Your website is your front line, customer facing salesperson. If you wouldn't keep a crappy and unproductive salesperson, why would you keep a crappy unproductive website? As a result, we have to conduct a performance review of your online "salesperson".

Your website is where you're supposed to be making money. The problem is, a lot of websites make buying difficult. Let me say that again: It's very easy to make buying difficult. This happens all the time because we're not paying attention to how the consumer goes through the buying process. We're so busy putting a bunch of stuff up for sale on our websites that we forget whom that stuff is there for. So, we have to examine whether your website is making it difficult for the consumer to buy.

Now, you might look at your website and say, "its always been that way, we've never had a problem with it!" YOU might not be having a problem with it but the consumer might be! The technology that consumers are using today (i.e., desktops, laptops, tablets, mobile devices, etc.) is changing rapidly and if the technology of your website is not consistent with the consumers' technology, say "goodbye" to your customers. It needs to be as easy as possible for the consumer to buy something from you and that means "one click and you're done"! So, what questions do we need to ask?

Can the user see your website on their mobile device? An increasing number of people are shopping using their mobile devices and the number is only going to increase with time, so you need to address this now. Most website platforms today automatically adjust for mobile devices (meaning, they are laid out in a way that makes it easy for the consumer to look at and navigate your website. If you're using an old platform OR you've had your website for several years, you're likely to have problems. That's when you look like you're in the stone ages and it can mean your visitors won't even bother trying to see what's on your website.

Are all the links on your website working? It's critical that you fix your broken links because if someone comes to your website and clicks on something and it doesn't take them where they thought they were going, they're going to click away from your website. You can use this website http://www.brokenlinkcheck.com/ to have all of the links on your website checked in just a few minutes.

It's free and you don't have to sign up for it. If this particular link doesn't work (which it should), then you can do a Google search for "broken link checker" and you'll see several options pop up.

Are you making the user click through a bunch of pages just to get to the item they're looking for? If so, you're going to say "goodbye" to them. This also happens when you prevent them from quickly accessing what they want on your site because you're so busy throwing pop-ups at them asking them to sign up for your newsletter or to answer a survey or some such thing.

How much stuff are you presenting to the consumer on your home page? We often put so much information and products on our home page that it's overwhelming to the consumer. As a result, you need to make some decisions for the consumer at the outset. This means you decide what to present to them so they think those are the only things available for them to consider. So, instead of offering ten options, pick the three that are the best and then display those. If they're interested in the three, they're likely to spend more time roaming your website to see what else you have to offer. Always remember, the more options you offer, the more reasons you're giving the consumer to click away. Too many choices are a bad thing on websites!

Do you know what people are doing on your site? I don't mean are they buying or not. It's understanding if your website is creating a problem for the consumer to get what they want. One way to determine what people are doing is with "Google Analytics". Google Analytics is a tracking program that Google provides to anyone with a website. If you have someone managing your website, it's likely that Google Analytics is already installed on your site. If not, it's something you need to have installed and if you don't want to do it yourself (it's actually very easy) you can have it installed by someone from a website called Fiverr.com where for $5, they'll install it for you. You may also want to ask them to give you a brief tutorial of Google Analytics.

Google Analytics will tell you how long your visitors are on your site once they arrive. If they are leaving the site right after arriving, you know you've got a problem with whatever they're seeing immediately upon arriving at your site. You can also see what pages your visitors are clicking on when they visit your site. If they aren't spending time visiting other pages on your site, it means they haven't seen anything compelling enough for them to spend more time. It also includes how they arrived at your site, meaning the website they were on immediately before arriving at your site. These are your "referral" sites. For example, they might be coming from Facebook or from a blog that someone wrote about your product or from some other publication you've been written up in or from a Google search or electronic press release. Knowing where your visitors are coming from can help you determine your best source of website traffic and help you decide where to concentrate your marketing resources and attention. Once you start using Google Analytics, you'll be amazed at how much more in control you'll feel about your situation because now you'll have the data that points you in the direction you need to go.

ANOTHER WAY YOUR WEBSITE IS PROBABLY KILLING YOUR SALES

First impressions matter! Once someone arrives at your website, you can only expect to have their attention for about two seconds before they click away. That's the amount of time it takes for a person to view the top of a website and determine whether or not they want to spend any more time there. It's also likely that the visitor may not ever scroll down your site or click anywhere else. As a result, what shows up at the top of your website has to communicate everything you want the visitor to know about your product. In a way, the top portion of your website has to be treated like a giant billboard. It's advertising space. It screams something. It's not about describing a product and all it's features and benefits and showing a bunch of products. It's where you make a compelling sales pitch to the visitor that makes them feel like they want or need or have to have your product.

Let me give you an example to help you to better understand what I mean. Think about when you go into the grocery store. Let's say you're walking down the laundry detergent aisle, or shampoo for that matter. You notice shelves filled to capacity with products, most of the same shape and size, varying mostly in color. At this point, you don't even know which product is which. Then you start looking more closely and the first thing you look for is something familiar. With all the choices available, you're looking for the easiest way to select your detergent because you're busy and want to get out of the store so you can get on with your day. In most cases, you're looking at the brand name because you, like everyone else, buy products based on brand name. It's not that your brand is any better than the rest of the detergent on the shelf, it's that the company that makes your brand has done the best job advertising to you. As a result, when standing in the grocery aisle looking for detergent, you're going to buy their brand. Now, if the store is out of your brand, you then have to spend more time trying to figure out which of the rest of them you might want to buy. You're still motivated by the same things: you need detergent and you want to get out of the store as quick as possible but how do you choose? You start by looking at the brand names to see if there is anything else remotely familiar to you. If not, you then look at how the product is described below the large brand name. This is usually presented in what we call a "tagline", a short one-sentence description of the product that will hopefully make you want to buy it if this is the only information you have about it. So, for example, here are the taglines of some of the most popular brands of laundry detergent:

"Adds brightness to whites."

"Clean clothes for dirty work.

"Committed to your health and the environment."

"Fast. Reliable. Affordable."

"Gets clothes cleaner than any other soap."

"Longer life for prints."

"No other soap like it."

"Protect them before they fade."

"Protects the sensitive skin of babies."

"So kind to hands."

"Stronger than dirt."

"To smell it is to love it."

"Truly a miracle of mildness."

"Wash more loads of clothes."

"We care for the clothes you wear."

"White without bleaching."

When you look at this list, think about it, if the brand you're most familiar with wasn't available, which of these taglines would resonate with you most? The one that resonates most is the one you're going to end up buying. We, as consumers, are motivated to solve our problems quickly, so companies need to make it as easy as possible for people to buy, which is why what you see on a label in a store is so important.

This same thing applies to shopping on the Internet. When people get to a website, they want to see something familiar. It doesn't have to be a famous product or brand name; it just has to be familiar in some way. So that means the top of your website, much like entering the laundry detergent aisle, has to present something that makes the consumer stop in their tracks, click on that product and buy.

If you have a product that solves a problem for the consumer, you'll be miles ahead of everyone else. As a result, you will use your "billboard" to state what the consumer's problem is and how your product solves that problem. If your product doesn't solve a problem for them, then you will have to get really creative about how you present it to them. Recognize that if all you're doing is presenting a bunch of products for people to look at, they may as well click away from your site because you aren't giving them any reason to buy and you aren't telling them you want them to buy.

In this situation, you have to create an emotion in the consumer that leaves them feeling like they'll be a better person if they buy your product. Maybe they'll have a better life or perhaps they'll be prettier or more handsome if they buy your product. Maybe it's as simple as saying something like "you deserve a treat today!" You have to connect your product with some emotion in the consumer because once you tap into their emotions they will be less resistant to buying from you.

So, let's take a look at your website for a moment. Go ahead and look at it. What do you see? Is there a visually compelling image that evokes a feeling in you or is it just a bunch of products staring you in the face? Do you see anything that makes you feel like they're talking about the problem you have? Does the website say anything to you in big bold print that makes you feel like they're talking to you? Is there anything that asks you to do something? When you look at your own website, how do you feel about it as a consumer? Is it boring? Do you feel like there's any compelling reason for you to? Probably not.

In the next section, I'm going to give you an example of how this works but for right now, let me just say the following: there are three things you have to have at the top of your website if you expect to keep people on your site when they arrive there: (1) a visually compelling image, (2) a provocative caption or "tag line" which is a line of text that is referencing the image in some way and (3) a "call to action" ("CTA"). A call to action tells the consumer what you want them to do when they're on your website. Examples are: "Buy Now", "Sign Up Now", and "Get Your Discount Now". It's really simple: if you don't ask for the sale, you're less likely to get it!

If you can successfully incorporate the three items from above, you're likely to see an increase in the amount of time people are spending on your website AND your "bounce rate" is likely to go down. You can find this bounce rate in your Google Analytics account. The bounce rate is the percentage of your website visitors that land on your home page but never go anywhere else on the site after they get there. If you're going through a huge exercise of driving traffic to your website, you cannot have people clicking away from your site once they get there. Once you address these issues with your website, you can see if your visitors are spending more time on your site and whether that corresponds to an increase in sales.

YOUR "BILLBOARD"
IN ACTION

So, let's take a look at that example now. Let's say you're in the business of selling weight loss products. The last thing you want to be doing is putting a bunch of weight loss product photos on your home page because really, who gives a shit?! People are inundated with messages and ads about losing weight like "Lose Weight Now" and "Click Here if you want to lose 30 lbs!" and all that crap. NO ONE responds to messaging like that. If this is what you're doing with your website, I can tell you with certainty that this is having a negative impact on your sales. So, if this is the product you're trying to sell, what you want to do at the tope of your website is get an image of a woman in a beautiful wedding dress and use a caption that says "How Would You Like To Fit Into That Dress Again?" and then the CTA might be "Click Here to find out how". THAT is how you sell weight loss products! Why? Because when you think about weight loss products, most of them are targeting women. So you think to yourself, at what point in a woman's life is she going to be at what she considers to be her ideal weight? It's her wedding day! From the day she gets married forward, it's likely she will begin gaining weight and that is why you're in business selling weight loss products. What we're doing here is connecting the weight loss products with the positive emotion associated with how the woman felt about herself and her weight on her wedding day. We're then offering the promise that she could be that weight again if she buys this product.

Now, if she's gotten a divorce along the way, then the messaging may change to something like "How Would You Like To Fit Into That Dress Again And Get The Ultimate Revenge", which is to stick it to the ex-husband who was probably ragging on her the whole time about her weight! Yeah, I know it's a stereotype but you're in the business of selling and you have to use whatever will work to increase your sales.

ARE YOU SHOUTING THE LOVE?

Now that we've addressed (and hopefully overcome) the issues with your website, we need to look at how you can make your website do more for you. This happens in the form of customer testimonials or reviews on the site. If your website provider doesn't give you the ability to put reviews on your site, then you need to investigate a different provider. It's important to understand that customer reviews are one of the main reasons that people will choose your product over someone else's. Testimonials serve to confirm that a product is as advertised and as also the experience that a customer has had with both the product and the company. This is something we call "social proof". When shopping online, we have no way to experience the product first hand so we have to rely on others to tell us what it's like.

If you don't currently have customer testimonials on your site and some that are prominently displayed, you need to spend some time collecting those testimonials.

Most people are afraid to ask their customers for testimonials because they feel like they're imposing on them. The reality is, you NEED those testimonials because they will help you sell more products. In order to get your customer testimonials, you have to ask them for it. You don't necessarily have to offer them anything in exchange. You just have to ask if they'd be willing to provide you with one. If you have a good relationship with your customers, it should be easy to get some of them to write something for you.

When asking your customers for testimonials, you're actually helping yourself in another way. You'll be gathering information about your product that you might not otherwise be aware of. So, in order to get your customer testimonials, ask them the following questions:

1. Can you think of anything that might have prevented you from purchasing this product? If so, what would that have been?

2. Once you bought the product, what was your reaction to it?

3. Was there anything specific about the product that you liked the most?

4. Are there two or three other benefits you can describe about the product?

5. If you were to recommend the product to someone else, what would you say?

So, let's explore each of these more closely. The first question you're asking is trying to get at what objections the customer might have had prior to the actual purchase. If they can recall what they were thinking going into the purchase, you can use this information as the basis for making some changes to your website, product or marketing that can overcome these objections before they arise.

The second question gets at why the customer felt it was worth it to buy your product. It explains what the product had to have to make it worth it for them to overcome their objections.

The third question identifies what the customer liked the most about your product. This may be the same answer as number two. You can use this information to further emphasize the most important aspect of the product in your product descriptions, on your website, and your marketing.

The fourth question gets at the other things your customer likes about the product. These are the other things they liked but weren't the top reason they bought the product.

The last question gets you any additional information the customer might share with you. This may be where they share information with you about your great customer service or how quickly the product arrived.

When you put all of the answers together you not only have great information for your testimonial, but you have great market research that can help you to make changes in what you're presenting to the consumer online and that is certain to help you.

When you have testimonials or reviews, they should be prominently displayed on the home page of your website. If you can incorporate them into your website "billboard", all the better because your customer's voice is the best endorsement for your product and something that the consumer relies on in their purchasing decisions.

"LANDING" THOSE SALES

Now we move completely away from your website to some of the ways you can improve your sales. One thing that happens when you're selling online is that you have to get people to give you their email addresses even if they haven't bought from you. The reason you do this is because people on your email list are considered "warm leads". They are the ones most likely to buy your products and it doesn't cost anything to maintain your communication with them while they're deciding on when they're going to buy from you. As a result, you have to treat your email list like a sales engine.

So, if email addresses can generate new sales, how do you go about getting those emails? Most emails come from purchases made in the past. The problem is, if people have bought from you already, they might not be ready to buy again any time soon. Others come from email signup forms on websites. The problem is email signup forms on websites tend to perform poorly so what are you supposed to do?

Getting email addresses is not a passive thing. You can't just expect someone to hand over their email address. You have to give them something of value in exchange.

The most common and successful approach to getting email addresses is through the use of "landing pages". These are standalone website pages usually generated by a third-party provider such as LeadPages.com or Unbounce.com or Instapage.com. You can also set them up on your own website but that will require a lot more work so it's not a first choice. These third party providers have templates that you can use which makes it really easy to start capturing email addresses. The templates contain a lot of language in them that have been tested and proven to produce the best results.

You landing page will be made up of the following things: (1) an offer of something of value such as discount coupons, e-books, limited time offers, contest entry, free trials or demos, downloads or a special video that has valuable information in it and the only way the visitor can watch it is if they provide their email address. A lot of digital products are sold this way, (2) a photo of the offer, (3) a compelling description of the offer, (4) a call to action, and (5) and a clickable call to action button.

So, let me give you an example of what a typical landing page looks like. Let's say you're a book author and trying to build your email list. You have (1) your offer which is a free e-book that will be available for download (or sent via email) once the visitor provides their email address, (2) a photo of the e-book, (3) a compelling description of the offer (e-book) such as "The Pages Turn Themselves", (4) your call to action which is "To get your copy of this page turner, tell me where to send it" and (5) clickable call to action button that says "Get My Free Book NOW".

Here's another example. Let's say you're a travel agent. Your landing page would consist of the following: (1) your offer is the chance to win a free vacation, (2) you show a photo of a beautiful travel destination, (3) you describe the offer as "Win The Vacation Of Your Dreams!", (4) your call to action is "Hurry, Only A Limited Time Offer and (5) a clickable call to action button that says "Click Here To Enter".

Once you have your landing page set up to capture emails, you have to make sure that the page is integrated with your email provider. The third party landing page providers I suggested in this section will provide you direction on how to do this.

So now, you're all set and ready for those emails. The next thing that happens is you have to drive traffic to those landing pages. This is typically done through some form of advertising be it Facebook ads or Google search ads. I'll be getting into both of these advertising platforms in a later section of the book so for right now, just know that once you start capturing email addresses via these landing pages, you're going to increase your ability to generate sales with a lot less work.

ARE YOU PESTERING PEOPLE WITH EMAILS?

I know that when you just read the title of this section, you thought to yourself "heavens no, I don't want to piss people off!" If that's how you responded, then you need to smack yourself in the head for being so polite. You're not in business to be polite, you're in business to make money and your email list is there for you to make money from.

Let me give you an example: have you ever heard of an online lending company, Kabbage? They have a website that allows you to enter a little bit of information about your business and in a very short amount of time; they tell you if you've qualified for a small business loan. It's really slick looking, very quick to apply and *poof* you've got money for your small business. It's a completely legitimate business and one that I've used to get a small business loan. (NOTE: this is NOT an endorsement for them and/or any other online lender. I have serious issues with these companies so research them very carefully if you decide it's something you might want to pursue.) The thing with Kabbage is, if you've ever applied for a loan with them or you've signed up for their emails, you will find them emailing you every business day! Not kidding,

I get emails from them every business day, sometimes more than once a day. Since it's easier to click "delete" than to go through the trouble of unsubscribing from their email list, you are going to see Kabbage emails in your inbox every business day ad nausea. The reason they do this is because they know you might not need or want a loan today but if the day comes that you do need a loan, you'll think of them. They do this because it's very effective.

If you're not doing everything you can to build your email list and you're not emailing the people on your list as often as possible, then you're missing the opportunity to maintain the relationships you already have with those people. You're also missing out on an entirely new group of people to sell to and you're missing out on an opportunity to sell to people who are already interested in your business or product. Your email list is like the equivalent of printing money. Go ahead, try it! Offer some kind of special to your email list and see if you don't generate sales from it. Remember, the people on your email list are the easiest people to sell to. They already like you and they're already willing to buy from you. Now all you have to do is TELL them you want them to buy from you. Also, remember, if you've spent any money advertising to get people on your email list, you're throwing your money away if you don't capitalize on that email list. Don't let your list go stagnant just because you think you're bothering people.

Now, just to be clear, I want to make sure you understand that the emails I'm talking about right now are very different from the ones you set up for when people abandon their shopping carts. Those emails are specific to getting them to finalize their purchases. The emails I'm talking about here are ones you use to cultivate and nurture the relationships you have with the people on your list. If they keep seeing emails in their inbox, they will remember that you're there. When they ARE ready to buy something like what you have to offer, they're likely to buy from you before anyone else.

To do this, you create and set up a series of automatically scheduled emails in your email program (we're talking MailChimp, aWeber, Constant Contact, Infusionsoft and any of the other major email programs, NOT Gmail or other personal email service with your address book). These are emails that you schedule to be delivered over a long period of time (could be a month or longer).

When you send out a series of emails to people, you have to send them information that's going to be beneficial to them and that means that you are not talking about your products all the time. In fact, this series of emails will rarely make reference to your product, if at all. People want to have a relationship with you. They want to feel like they know you. They want to hear your "voice". Once they feel like they have some level of trust in you, they become invested in you and that's when they're less resistant to emails and offers that talk about your product. It's also a time when, if they're going to buy your product, they will.

Now, one thing that gets people in a tizzy is the question of what these emails should say. You always have to remember, you do not talk about you rather you talk about THEM. It's all about them. It's all about making them feel like you care about them.

One of the ways we show people on our email list that we care about them is to send them helpful information. There are websites on the Internet that you can use for ideas of content to send to your email list. Some of these include: buzzsumo.com, paper.li, and getpocket.com. You want to look for interesting or funny stories, or perhaps a great "human interest" story. These are always great things to share with people on your list. Remember, the whole point is for you to make people connect with you while you're waiting for the moment they're going to be ready to buy.

If you don't have time to find the content yourself, you can always hire someone from Fiverr.com and for only $5, you can have him or her write the content for you. Just make sure you're specific with them about the kind of content you want them to write.

Finally, let me just give you an example of what one of these emails might look like. Let's say you're in the business of selling yoga clothing. And let's say you're not one of the major brands that sell yoga clothing. You've got your work cut out for you because it's such a competitive market. You have a loyal customer base and you need to make sure those customers remain loyal to you and also become your brand ambassadors. Here is how you might write an email to them during the time you're waiting for them to buy something from you:

Email Subject Line: "Five Ways To Pass The Time In The Grocery Line"

Email Content: "We all know that there are just certain stores we shop in that take forever to get out of. We stand in line for so long that our hair has grown an inch and now we have to go to the salon that will take up even MORE of our time! Well, now you can benefit from that time in line, shorten your yoga workout and have a great hairstyle by the time you're out of there! And to help you, we're giving you some of the best yoga poses for standing in line at the store."

At this point in the email, you would insert photos of actual yoga poses that might work while standing in line. Or, you could insert funny photos of dogs doing yoga poses.

You then continue the email by saying:

"This message brought to you by the company that knows your time is valuable, your body even more so and a sense of humor about how ridiculous things can be in life!

Stay tuned for the next installment of kooky things that go on in life!

Sincerely,

Your friend standing next to you in line

If you've tried our groovalicious yoga wear, we'd love to have you review it at (insert link to where they can provide a review)

If you think we're a really cool company, forward this email to a friend and tell your friends on social media.

Like us on Facebook at: (insert your Facebook page address)

Insert your website here

Insert your company contact information here"

What you see happening in this email is you're providing the people on your list with something that's entertaining (or the content could be informational), it doesn't take life too seriously, it recognizes the challenges people can have, it names those challenges and offers some kind of solution, none of which has anything to do with your product. You've giving the reader a sense of your personality and making them feel like they might want you as a friend. You're also asking them to do something (a call to action). You're asking for a review. You're asking them to tell other people about you. You're asking them to check you out on social media and letting them know where they can find you with your website and contact information.

You would be amazed at how effective emails like this can be. They can push people over into the "buy" category simply because they resonate with the people on your list. It can make them more receptive to getting a future email from you that invites them to check out a new product that you have or take advantage of a special deal you're running. This is how you continue communicating with people on your email list while you're waiting for them to buy because they are most definitely what we call "warm leads". Once you manage to get people on your list, you have to keep them warm until they're finally ready to buy.

TRAFFIC ON THE FREEWAYS AND TOLL ROADS

When you think about the world you live in, that of selling online, success boils down to making people aware that you're there. A large part of that success is getting people to your website so they can buy. This is called "website traffic". If you don't have website traffic, then you have no sales, plain and simple. So, your goal has to be to generate as much website traffic as you can.

There are two ways to generate traffic. One is free and one requires those advertising dollars. Here is an example to help you conceptualize this.

You have to look at your website traffic the same way you look at road traffic, there are freeways and toll roads and you can take either one to your destination. If you choose the freeway, you're going to be faced with a lot of other drivers out there clogging up the road, slowing you down and getting in your way. They might even make it impossible for you to make any forward progress. At a minimum, it takes you a long time to get to your destination.

Toll roads, on the other hand, get you to your destination really quick. There are fewer people there, fewer distractions and if you're really clever, you can always be out in front of everyone else. Selling on the Internet is just like this. There are free ways and paid ways. The free methods are called "organic traffic" and the paid is rightly called "paid traffic". They're both important in your efforts to increase your sales, but one will get you to your destination a whole lot faster. So, let's explore both of these "roads".

THE FREEWAY – ORGANIC TRAFFIC

Organic traffic is a great source of free traffic. It is traffic that originated elsewhere on the Internet, usually in the form of links from other pages. One way organic traffic is generated is when someone references your product or website on their blog. They would likely put a link in the story that connects to your website. Social media also generates free traffic. So, if you've got a lot of people on your social media accounts like Facebook, Twitter, Pinterest, Instagram, YouTube and so forth, you can place links on those sites to make it easy for people to click over to your website.

Writing is another method that develops organic traffic. Blog posts that you write, either on your site or as a guest on another person's blog, will generate free traffic. When someone reads your post, they might reference it on their own website or social media accounts which means you might get traffic from someone else's followers. Issuing press releases generates traffic, just make sure to include website links in them. The emails you send will generate a significant amount of free traffic. You need to always include a website link in your emails so your readers can quickly click over to your website. Most of the time you can accomplish this by adding your website to your signature block.

Finally, a lot of free traffic to your website will come from people searching for things on search engines like Google. They'll be searching for something specific and your website will pop up in their search results. Keep in mind that there are a lot of factors that influence whether your website shows up in someone's Google search so it's not always the case that someone is going to see you there. More about this in a minute ...

Organic traffic is very beneficial in your efforts to increase your sales. The problem, as you can see from the examples above, is that you have to do a lot of work to put content out on the Internet for people to see. This means blog posts, social media posts, press releases, emails, articles you might write for other publications, interviews you do with online journalists, and reaching out to people who can generate more organic traffic for you. You can see that this could be a full time job and the reality is, your full time job is running your business. As a result, you need an alternative to help you get those sales sooner rather than later and most important, with far less work. This is where your advertising comes in.

THE TOLL ROAD – ONLINE ADVERTISING

I know you might be saying to yourself right now that you don't have any money for advertising but let me say this, when your sales are declining, what you need to do more than anything else is spend MORE on advertising! An increase in spending on advertising (provided it's in the right place) is going to be the most productive and quickest way for you to increase your sales.

The most effective place to spend your advertising dollars is on the Internet. Not only is it the most effective in reaching the largest number of people, but you can also track it. As a result, you always know how your ads are performing and whether you're generating any sales associated with that particular ad or method. Other forms of advertising such as traditional media channels like print, television, radio, newspapers, etc. may be productive but the problem is that there is almost no way to track the performance of those ads. You don't know who is reading what and you don't know if anyone is actually coming to your website (or buying for that matter) as a result of any advertising that you do in those channels.

So, let's take a look at how this works. While there are many ways that you can advertise online, the two most productive are Google search ads and Facebook ads.

Google search ads are the advertisements that pop up as people search for keywords on the Google page. They are most effective for products that can be easily described by specific keywords. For example, if you have a product whose search keyword is "yoga pants", Google search ads can be really productive for you because anyone who is doing a search on Google for yoga pants is probably going to type in those exact words. As a result, your ad will be shown to these people (assuming there aren't a lot of advertisers using that keyword for their ads) who are specifically looking for yoga pants right now. It's likely that they will click on your ad, which will take them to your website, thereby increasing the likelihood that you might get a sale from that person.

If you have a hard time determining appropriate keywords for your product, you can "borrow" the keywords from similar products. Go to the website Spyfu. com and type in the website address of a company selling similar products to see what keywords they are using for their advertising on Google search. This will give you some ideas for what you can start with in determining the keywords you should use if you plan to use Google search ads. For $5, you can also hire someone experienced with Google search from Fiverr.com to help you develop your keyword list.

Now, as exciting as it might seem for you to be able to run some Google search ads to people who are ready to buy right now, there may be a problem. You have to keep in mind that your ads are not necessarily going to be on the first page of the search results. Your placement is dependent upon how much competition there is for the keywords that are relevant to your product. If there's a lot of competition from other higher paying advertisers, you could find your ad showing up on the second or third page.

Most consumers won't search beyond the first page of results. Getting your ad on the first page is going to get very expensive very quick. As your competition may be much bigger than you and have more money, they won't spare any expense to get their ads on the first page. You can actually look on Spyfu.com to see how much they're spending each month. As a result, slogging it out with your competition for Google search ads may not be your best path to success. So, you need to be judicious about your decision to use Google search ads for your business.

If you find that Google search ads are not the most economical or productive for you, then you should consider advertising with Facebook. Facebook advertising is probably the least expensive and most productive form of online advertising. As of this writing, there are 1.6 billion Facebook users and that means, depending upon whom you want to show your ad to, you can select any or all of those users. Obviously, you're not going to advertise to 1.6 billion people BUT you certainly have access to them!

One of the advantages of using Facebook advertising is its flexibility. Facebook gives you several options for your ads based on what you're trying to accomplish. So, for example, you might want to use ads to send traffic to your website, if you sell mobile apps, you can advertise for people to download those apps, you can let people know that you have a special event taking place and give them an easy way to sign up for your event, you can create a special offer such as discounts or other rewards and make it easy for people to claim that special offer, you can advertising video demonstrations of your products or a customer testimonial or use a video that is designed to attract their attention in some way, you can create local awareness for your product if it's geographically based, you can use slideshows and show multiple products at the same time in your ad. As such, you have a wide range of options for how and what you advertise to people on Facebook.

Another advantage of Facebook advertising is that it's an easy way to identify people that might be interested in your product. That could mean your existing customers, people who have "self-identified" on Facebook as people who have bought other similar products and might be interested in yours, people who are interested in a product like yours but have not yet been made aware of you, and people who don't yet know they want or need your product. You can target all of these people with your Facebook ads and that means you have a significantly larger relevant population to advertise to and therefore generate sales from.

Before you start advertising on Facebook, you need to make sure that your Facebook cover photo is set up using the same criteria as your website and landing pages: compelling image, provocative text and a call to action. Once your cover photo is set, then you can start your advertising.

Facebook advertising involves the following basic things: (1) an ad campaign that includes one or more ads, (2) ads that have compelling images, provocative text and calls to action, (3) determining where you want people to go when they click on your Facebook ad, be it your website, your landing page or your e-commerce site, (4) deciding who you want to see your ad, i.e. your "target audience" (the most likely people to want or need your product), (5) deciding how much money you want to spend each day and then (6) submitting your ad to Facebook for approval.

Of all of these things, the one that has the greatest impact on the success of your ads and enables you to spend the least amount of money is #4, what we call "ad targeting". Ad targeting simply means determining who is going to see your ads. This is something that you will determine with the help of Facebook.

Facebook ad targeting allows you to select people based on various criteria. So, for example, you can select people based on gender, age, where they live, what kind of job they have, how much money they make, whether or not they own a home, their marital status, whether or not they have children, how old their children are and so forth.

Now, you might think this is all you need to start advertising, but you need to be careful of the relevance of your target audience. Lets say you've targeted married women, ages 25-34 and who live in Los Angeles. You could certainly advertise to this group but what does this information tell you about what these people are likely to buy and more important, whether they might be interested in your product? It doesn't tell you anything. As a result, we have to get more specific in our targeting. This is where Facebook, the "gatherer of all things data", gives you the jackpot.

Facebook enables you to target your advertising based on the things people have clicked "like" on. Every time a person clicks "like", Facebook puts that user into its database as someone who is interested in a particular thing. So, if a user has clicked "like" on a fashion designer that sells really expensive clothing, Facebook will put that user into the database of people who like fashion and who also like things that are expensive. Facebook does this to every one of their 1.6 billion users and, as a result, has a huge database of categorized potential customers. They then provide all of this data to you as an advertiser and they provide you with an easy way of identifying people that might make the most sense for your product.

The reason these "likes" are important to you for your advertising on Facebook is the assumption that, if someone clicks "like" on a certain Facebook page, they're either an existing customer of that product or they are going to be interested in Facebook pages and products that are similar. As a result, you can target people who have clicked "like" on all of the Facebook pages of products similar to your own. If they've bought a similar product in the past, it's possible that they might be interested in buying yours in the future if only they knew you were out there.

Let me show you how this might work for you. For my example lets assume that you sell weight loss products. You can target people based on whether they've clicked "like" on other weight loss products, such as Weight Watchers, Jenny Craig, etc. You can also target people who have expressed an interest in the famous personal trainers from TV shows about people losing weight (i.e., "Biggest Loser"), people who've expressed an interest in fitness equipment, people who are interested in diabetes or people interested in authors who have become famous because of how much weight they've lost.

Here's another example of how this ad targeting works. If you selling home-related goods, let's say you're an interior designer or you sell lamps, you need to think about who might need and want these products. The most obvious person is a homeowner because homeowners spend a lot of money on products and services related their homes. Facebook gives you the ability to target just those people who are homeowners, but be aware that not every homeowner has been identified as such in Facebook. As a result, you need to find the rest of the homeowners who "self identify" on Facebook as being homeowners.

People indirectly reveal their homeownership status is by clicking "like" (meaning, expressing an interest in) on things that are associated with a home. So, that might include landscaping, garden designers, home improvement stores, home improvement television shows, or magazines that pertain to the house such as Architectural Digest. This same example would also apply to real estate agents and mortgage brokers. Both are looking for people who want to buy or sell a home and so they could target the exact same audience as the seller of home-related goods.

When you target people on Facebook in this way, you're telling Facebook, "only show my ad to people who have expressed an interest in these things". As a result, Facebook will dramatically narrow your target audience, leaving you with an audience that is already predisposed to be interested in your product. Because it's a more narrowly targeted audience, you'll end up spending significantly less and you're more likely to generate sales.

Now, there is one last thing I need to point out before we move on and that is, just because you advertise to someone does not mean they are going to buy the instant they see your ad. Everything depends both on you the kind of product you have and also whether the consumer needs or wants your product at that moment. As such, you have view your advertising with a longer range in mind. You need to be advertising on a regular basis because you need to be in front of the consumer and "top of mind" at the point they're ready to buy. What will happen is, when they are finally ready, they will remember you because they've been seeing a steady flow of ads from you. Thanks to consistent advertising, you are familiar to them. There is an increased likelihood that they will buy from you rather than someone else.

CHASING PEOPLE AROUND THE INTERNET – WE DO IT BECAUSE IT WORKS!

Now, we have to talk about what happens when you have the right ad and the right target audience for your ad, but you're not seeing any sales right away. You have to allow for the fact that you may be selling a product that people don't want or need at the moment they see your ad. As a result, what we do is something called "retargeting". You may not know what this is by its name but I can assure you, if you've ever shopped online or even clicked on a product online, you've experienced it.

This is how it works. When you go to a website and click on a product, you will often see that same product showing up later on in several different places while you're searching the Internet. This is what's called "retargeting" advertising. The retargeting ads are triggered if you don't buy the first time you click on a product online and will continue displaying everywhere you go on the Internet for some period of time. It could be for a few days, a few weeks or even a month. It's really annoying but the reality is, these ads are among the most effective ads of any on the Internet. In fact, there was one statistic I read that said these retargeting ads were eight times more likely to generate a sale than the original ad. As a result, this is something you should be actively pursuing because you can see a dramatic increase in your sales.

Facebook provides you with the ability to set up these retargeting ads and as of the printing of this book, there were two third-party major platforms that allow you to do retargeting: PerfectAudience.com and Adroll.com. One thing to keep in mind, the retargeting ads you set up in Facebook only allow you to retarget people on Facebook. The third-party providers enable you to chase people all over the Internet, no matter where they go. It's definitely worth looking into for your business.

I should note that if you are selling directly to Amazon. com, they will do the retargeting ads for you. It's done automatically so there's nothing you need to do to make this happen. Just know that you're paying a whopping fee to Amazon for all the services including this one. Recognize that if Amazon is doing this kind of advertising on your behalf, it becomes increasingly less likely that people are ever going to land on your website. You have to decide what's best for you and your business as sometimes "doing a deal with the devil" is not always a bad thing. In my case, it was a bad thing and that's why I walked away from Amazon.

IS THERE AN UGLY TRUTH HERE?

Now, this next issue is something that no business owner or entrepreneur wants to even consider when examining why their product isn't selling. Every one of us has spent years and countless dollars developing and bringing our products to market and no one wants to consider that the decline in sales or the fact that the sales never really took of is related to that there is just something wrong with the product. I know it's hard to think about that, but you have to accept the reality that your product may have worked for the consumer in the past, but it isn't working anymore today.

It could be that your product no longer has a market or that the market is so small that you've exhausted the potential to sell your product. It's possible that your product is in a market that's so competitive; you simply can't gain any traction. It's possible that your product is in a market that's saturated, which is different from competitive. A competitive market is one where people are actually selling and making money. In a saturated market, you're likely to have so many sellers that none of them are making much money, or any at all. What results from this is that there is so much "noise" out there, that the consumer can't even find your product.

I also need to point out, as an aside, that many products come to market without the proper market research to determine if that product is viable, meaning is there a market to sell it into with enough consumers that want or need to buy it. Unfortunately, if a product is not really viable, many people will still go forward with launching that product because they're so emotionally invested in it. Within a relatively short period of time, they're out of business. So, it's critical that you do your homework to ensure that the product you're bringing to market actually makes sense. Obviously, this is not only relevant to people just coming into the market BUT it applies to any new product you might be thinking about introducing.

WHEN THE LOVE IS GONE – REJECTION STINKS

Sometimes you will find that the consumer is no longer interested in your product. It's not that it's all about everyone else or the new bright, shiny object, it's just that the consumer has changed or simply moved on because of what's going on for them. It could even be a generational thing. When this happens, there's nothing you can do about it other than to work on finding a new audience for your product. That's where Facebook can be really helpful to you. Combined with the multitude of other social media platforms out there, you can easily carve out a new audience that wants or needs it.

Every product will eventually reach a point where the consumer isn't interested anymore and that is when you have to take a hard look at the product to determine whether there is any chance you can reactivate the consumers' interest in the product.

I'VE DONE EVERYTHING
AND IT'S STILL
NOT WORKING

To recap, you look at whether there are external forces impacting your sales, things that are out of your control. Then, you look at things you CAN control. If people are abandoning their shopping carts, you aggressively pursue them with emails to get them to go forward with their purchase. If your website, e-commerce site and/or landing pages are getting in the way of the consumer buying from you, you make sure they're presented visually in a compelling way so that the consumer is more likely to spend more time on your site. You squeeze your email list for every possible sale you can get out of it. You use Facebook to help you identify and target the best customer for your product. You then use Facebook ads to help you sell and also increase the size of your audience. You do as much advertising as you can and also make heavy use of retargeting ads. You then take an honest look at your product to confirm that it solves a problem and it addresses that problem in a way that the consumer thinks will help them and make sure all of your marketing about the product is driving that message home.

Once you've addressed all those things, if you find you're still not able to get any traction with your sales, now is when you're going to have to get really creative about how you look at your product. This is where you make a major shift in how you're going to present your product to the consumer.

WHEN ALL ELSE FAILS

Sometimes, all it takes is presenting your product to the consumer in a different way. How many times have you seen a company change the packaging on a product or change their company logo? In some cases, that's all it takes.

The Lays Potato Chip package, famous for its bright, shiny yellow and white sunburst, was initially used for the new Baked Lays potato chip product. Having little success selling the product (my guess is because everyone familiar with the original package associated it with greasy potato chips), Lays changed the packaging in a way that emphasized the "Baked" and introduced large sections of color on the bags that were taken from the most modern colors in contemporary design. All of a sudden the consumer thinks there's a new product out there. It has a cool looking package with a product that's maybe more healthy and makes clever use of modern colors. This resulted in Lays being able to access a segment of the population that wasn't previously eating greasy potato chips but might be interested in a healthier version of the chips. And so, new package, whole new audience!

The Target store is probably the most famous of all successful logo changes. At one point, the word "Target" was superimposed on top of the famous bulls-eye.

Up until that time, Target was just another department store. When Target eliminated the brand name from the bulls-eye and made the bulls-eye the logo, everything changed for them. It also helped that they had great ads featuring a really cool dog.

The reason I bring up these examples is because they demonstrate how a small design change can have a huge impact on a product or brand. Obviously the two examples I've given are from huge companies that have a lot of money to research and invest in repackaging or redesign. This may not be possible for a small company but the point is, to start thinking about how you're presenting your product to the public. This is especially important when your sales are declining. Basically what you have to do is make the consumer "see" you again.

For a small company, it might be that the next production of your product, you change the product packaging, and that could mean the external packaging or the container that the product comes in. Think about how many different bottle designs there are for perfume. Sometimes people will buy a certain perfume just because they like the bottle. Think about the various gift shops you go into. You see something in a really cute package and you buy the product even though you really don't need or want it. You make the purchase because the packaging or container resonates with you in some way. Before you know it, out comes your wallet.

If you simply can't afford to make any kind of changes to the product packaging, then this is where you can introduce something that doesn't cost you any money.

TIME TO GET PROVOCATIVE!

Whenever anyone hears the word "provocative", certain images or thoughts come to mind. Well, obviously we're not going to use any of those images or thoughts to reintroduce your product to the market. What we ARE going to do is capitalize on what "provocative" really means and that is: "to provoke".

Let me give you an example of how this works in a different context. Imagine you've been in a long-term relationship with someone. You've seen that person for years, even decades, and the way you see them is that they're just that person walking around your life in sweatpants all the time. You remember way back when you fell in love with them, they were the sharpest, best-dressed person oozing with charm and pizzazz. Fast-forward to where you are in that relationship and you almost can't remember seeing the person that way. Life has distracted you and now they're just someone walking around your house in holey sweatpants.

Then, one day, you get an invitation to a very important event and it's "black tie only". The two of you start getting dressed for the event. You walk out into the living room to present yourselves to one another and your eyes pop out of your head because you can't believe what you're seeing. There, standing before you, someone you've known and haven't "seen" for what seems like forever has appeared in a way that rocks your world! They have "provoked" your attention and your interest. THAT is what you have to do with your product. The consumer has fallen out of love with you and now you have to do the work to get your product in shape so they fall in love with you again.

Now, with all the "noise" that's out there in the world today, so much so that the consumer can't even process everything that is put in front of them, you have to figure out how you can put your product in that black tie outfit and get noticed.

THE STORY SELLS EVERY TIME!

One of the most successful ways companies get the consumer's attention is by presenting the product in a funny or emotional way. This is where the story of your product becomes most important. The story of your product is not about you, your journey to bringing that product to market, your family, or all the things you like to do.

The story of your product is the story you tell the consumer, the story that gets them excited about it, that makes them feel a connection to it, that makes them feel invested in it and most important, makes them want to buy it. (Note: when you tell the story of your product you do not talk about the features. People don't find features and benefits to be funny or emotional unless you can talk about them in a way that is. It's very rare for that to be successful so don't waste your time trying). Your story has to be something the consumer can relate to or will catch their eye. Maybe you can present your product to them in a way that is so different from the way they normally think about it, that you grab their attention. You present it in a way that's really novel, which makes them feel like they've never seen it before. This is what's provocative to the consumer. This is what gets them to take action. The easiest way to understand this is to simply do the unexpected!

One of the best examples I've ever seen of this being done is for a product called the Squatty Potty. The company's tag line is "Healthy Colon, Healthy Life". It's no wonder they were having a problem increasing their sales.

The product is designed to fix bad bathroom "posture", which is apparently associated with one's challenges in "going". As part of the video marketing the company was doing, they had a promotional video that included a bunch of charts and graphs and doctors' recommendations and the usual boring crap (no pun intended!). Enter the unicorn.

An animated video was created that was designed to completely change the public's perception of the product. After all, a squat stool is a squat stool and nothing's going to change that! So, the company created a video that changed everything. The video is entitled "This Unicorn Changed The Way I Poop". In the video you see the live action narrator dressed as a medieval prince, talking about how the Squatty Potty is a "foot stool fit for a constipated king," but available to anyone, not just "bloated lords and hemorrhoidal ladies". The entire time the princely narrator is talking, the animated unicorn is pooping rainbow colored soft-serve into ice cream cones and then the prince picks up one of the cones and proceeds to lick the rainbow colored soft-serve.

People were buying this product, not because they had to have it or needed it; they bought it because they saw a hilarious video that everyone was talking about on the Internet. They bought the product to send to their friends as a joke and the rest is history, millions in the bank. Boom!

Obviously, not everyone is going to be that clever and make a video that goes viral (meaning, to everyone on the Internet), but it's certainly something to aspire to. And, keep in mind, if you manage to have a video go viral like this one did, your search engine ranking is going to be right there on the first page! In fact, any kind of serious media coverage of a product can greatly impact your search engine ranking, which means more people are seeing your product (and potentially buying it). So it's important to do whatever you can to draw attention to your product.

Another example of presenting your product in a completely unexpected way is a Japanese company that created a language translation program that was cleverly stored in a small device about the size of a USB flash drive. They marketed it as a way of picking up girls in other countries. I won't get into how inappropriate this was, especially given the video they used, but suffice it to say, it caught the media's attention and when that happens, a lot of people suddenly discover the product. At the core, all they did was take a completely ordinary, boring product and tell a story that was simply an unexpected use for the product.

In these examples, you can see that the creators had a basic product that identified a problem and offered a solution. Their issue was that they couldn't make people aware of the products because they weren't the type that were "top of mind", meaning something a person would normally think about. The average consumer didn't find these products interesting or necessary. There might have been other products on the market that were more compelling or worked better or looked better. The net result is still the same: the consumer wasn't buying. Once these companies told an unexpected story of their products and the consumer caught wind of them, the consumer was able to "see" the products in a new way that would then motivate them to buy.

In these examples, these entrepreneurs looked at their products and figured out how to connect those products to something that was either funny or provocative. If you can use these examples as a basis for determining how you might associate your product with something unusual, you stand a much better chance of getting more awareness for your product. You're also more likely to see an increase in your sales.

At the end of the day, every consumer buys on emotion and if your product, your website, landing pages, emails, advertisements and your story do not effectively trigger emotions in the consumer, you will forever be struggling to generate sales.

Every product has the potential to be presented in a different way. You just have to try a lot of things to see what resonates with the consumer today. Keep in mind, the consumers' needs and wants are always changing so you have to be actively engaged in changing the way you present your product to them so your product always seems brand new. This is how you can take a product that's finished its normal life cycle and extract every possible last dollar out of it.

SO, LET'S RECAP WITH A ROADMAP

1. Determine if your decline in sales is in any way associated with factors that are outside your control. If that is the case, you may have to just sit tight and hold your breath until things change.

2. Check your website or e-commerce site's abandoned cart report to see who's been shopping but not buying. You will find this report in your website's reporting menu selection. If you can't find it, go to the Help tab at the top of the site and type in "abandoned cart" which should trigger information that will help you find this report. Email everyone who abandoned their shopping cart. The goal is to reengage them so they go forward with their purchase.

3. Set up a series of automatically scheduled emails that are triggered when someone abandons their cart. Once you write the emails, you will determine how much time you want to allow between when they abandoned the cart and when they receive each email. The goal of these emails is to get them to complete their purchase.

4. Examine the top of your website. What does it look like? Do not scroll down the page. Do this on your desktop on and your mobile device. Ask a friend or colleague to do the same with your website so you can see how it appears on multiple desktops, laptops and mobile devices including tablets and smartphones. Make sure you are showing a compelling image, provocative text and call to action at the top of the site. All of these things should be visible at the top on all computers and mobile devices.

5. If you are using landing pages to capture emails, the same rules apply. Look at the top of your computer screen and mobile device to see what the landing page looks like. Do not scroll down the page. Make sure you have a compelling image, provocative text and a call to action.

6. Create a series of emails that you will set up in your email program/platform. You can send one each day or you can spread them out over time. Each email should contain information that is considered useful, helpful, entertaining, humorous, personal or pertain to a "human interest" story. Make your "voice" clear in these emails so that people can begin to feel an emotional connection to you. This will reduce their resistance to buying from you. Make sure to include calls to action where you are asking them for reviews, forward the email to friends, tell their friends about you, to follow you on social media, to visit your website and also include your contact information.

7. Online advertising is critical to your success. Facebook advertising is likely to be the most productive for you. Make sure that you are targeting the right audiences for your product and plan to spend at least a small amount of money on your ads each day. Create your ad campaigns (or hire someone to do this for you), use compelling images, provocative text and calls to action in the ads. Monitor your ad results to determine what is and isn't working and make adjustments accordingly. Use retargeting ads to chase people around Facebook and the Internet.

8. Determine if the consumer has fallen out of love with your product. If so, either pivot into something else or get really creative about presenting your product in a new way or you have to consider the possibility that it's time to hang it up.

9. Create a new and compelling, completely unexpected story about your product that will reignite the fire in the consumers' bellies and make them want you again. Disrupt the consumers' expectations about your product so they can see your product with fresh eyes.

CONCLUSION

Without a doubt, anyone who owns a business will face a decline in the sales of their product at some point. It's my hope that the things I've talked about in this book will give you a better understanding of why your product might not be selling or selling as well as it has in the past. It is also my hope that you can implement the suggestions I've made and see success as a result. Whatever the case, we press on as entrepreneurs because that's what we know how to do. We encounter problems every day and we solve them. We have the fortitude to keep going against all odds. There are days when we wonder why we're doing what we're doing and other days when we're reminded of the answer. And at the end of the day, we wouldn't choose another life for anything because to be an entrepreneur is to be truly free. I wish you continued and great success in your business.

HELPFUL RESOURCES

I recognize that there is a lot to digest from this book and I thought it might be helpful to provide reference material to help you address specific issues you're having with increasing your sales.

WEBSITE AND E-COMMERCE PROVIDERS:

BigCommerce.com

Spotify.com

Magento.com

Volusion.com

OpenCart.com

PrestaShop.com

WooCommerce.com

WordPress.org

THIRD PARTY LANDING PAGE PROVIDERS:

LeadPages.com

Unbounce.com

InstaPage.com

EMAIL PROVIDERS:

aWeber.com

MailChimp.com

ConstantContact.com

Infusionsoft.com

Hubspot.com

ONLINE ADVERTISING:

Facebook.com/Business

Ads.Twitter.com

Ads.Pinterest.com

Instagram ads are done through Facebook

LinkedIn.com/ad/start

YouTube.com/yt/advertise

Google.com/ads/searchads/

THIRD PARTY AD RETARGETING PROVIDERS:

AdRoll.com

PerfectAudience.com

CONTENT PROVIDERS:

BuzzSumo.com

Paper.li

GetPocket.com

Scoop.it

Feedly.com

Storify.com

Curata.com

TrapIt.com

PearlTrees.com

MEASURING YOUR WEBSITE PERFORMANCE:

GoogleAnalytics.com

BROKEN WEBSITE LINK CHECKER:

BrokenLinkCheck.com

FINDING OUT WHO'S TALKING ABOUT YOU ONLINE:

Google.com/alerts

Mention.com

HootSuite.com

WHERE TO GET ANYTHING DONE FOR $5:

Fiverr.com

GREAT SITE TO HELP YOU WRITE BETTER:

CopyBlogger.com

SAMPLES HEADLINES FOR WEBSITES, LANDING PAGES, EMAILS AND ADS

CopyBlogger.com is a website that I visit daily for information about writing online. Here's an excerpt from one blog post that addresses headlines or captions you can use to trigger an emotion in the consumer. All you have to do is fill in the blank with words that are relevant to your product.

1. Who Else Wants [blank]?

- Who Else Wants a Great WordPress Theme?
- Who Else Wants a Higher Paying Job?
- Who Else Wants More Fun and Less Stress When on Vacation?

2. The Secret of [blank]

- The Secret of Successful Podcasting
- The Secret of Protecting Your Assets in Litigation
- The Secret of Getting Your Home Loan Approved

3. Here is a Method That is Helping [blank] to [blank]

- Here is a Method That is Helping Homeowners Save Hundreds on Insurance

- Here is a Method That is Helping Children Learn to Read Sooner

- Here is a Method That is Helping Bloggers Write Better Post Titles

4. Little Known Ways to [blank]

- Little Known Ways to Save on Your Heating Bill

- Little Known Ways to Hack Google's Gmail

- Little Known Ways to Lose Weight Quickly and Safely

5. Get Rid of [problem] Once and For All

- Get Rid of Your Unproductive Work Habits Once and For All

- Get Rid of That Carpet Stain Once and For All

- Get Rid of That Lame Mullet Hairdo Once and For All

6. Here's a Quick Way to [solve a problem]

- Here's a Quick Way to Get Over a Cold

- Here's a Quick Way to Potty Train Junior

- Here's a Quick Way to Backup Your Hard Drive

7. **Now You Can Have [something desirable] [great circumstance]**

- Now You Can Quit Your Job and Make Even More Money
- Now You Can Meet Sexy Singles Online Without Spending a Dime
- Now You Can Own a Cool Mac and Still Run Windows

8. **[Do something] like [world-class example]**

- Speak Spanish Like a Diplomat
- Party Like Paris Hilton
- Blog Like an A-Lister

9. **Have a [or] Build a [blank] You Can Be Proud Of**

- Build a Body You Can Be Proud Of
- Have a Smile You Can Be Proud Of
- Build a Blog Network You Can Be Proud Of

10. **What Everybody Ought to Know About [blank]**

- What Everybody Ought to Know About ASP
- What Everybody Ought to Know About Adjustable Rate Mortgages
- What Everybody Ought to Know About Writing Great Headlines

Source:

http://www.copyblogger.com/10-sure-fire-headline-formulas-that-work/

Published July 30, 2006, by Brian Clark

SAMPLE SLOGANS OR TAGLINES

Here are some of the best taglines used by the most recognized brands. They are reprinted here so that you have some examples to refer to when developing the tagline that applies to your product. A slogan or tagline is what you put at the top of your website.

- The road will never be the same. - Acura
- Stronger than dirt. - Ajax
- I can't believe I ate the whole thing. - Alka-Seltzer
- The relief goes on. - Allegra
- Doesn't your dog deserve Alpo? - Alpo Dog Food
- Works like a dream. - Ambien
- Something special in the air. - American Airlines
- Behold the power of cheese. - American Dairy Association
- Don't leave home without it. - American Express
- "For fast, fast, fast relief." - Anacin
- Think different. - Apple Computer
- Never follow. - Audi
- Bayer works wonders. - Bayer Aspirin

- We mean clean. - Bissell
- Life's messy. Clean it up! - Bissell
- Sheer driving pleasure. - BMW
- The ultimate driving machine. - BMW
- The quicker picker-upper. - Bounty
- "When you've got it, flaunt it." - Braniff Airlines
- Fill it to the rim with Brim. - Brim Decaffeinated Coffee
- "Hope, triumph, and the miracle of medicine." - Bristol-Myers Squibb Co.
- The way to fly. - British Airways
- The world's favorite airline. - British Airways
- Wassup?! - Budweiser
- The king of beers. - Budweiser
- It just tastes better. - Burger King
- Have it your way. - Burger King
- "Calgon, take me away." - Calgon Toiletries
- Between love and madness lies obsession. - Calvin Klein
- Nothing comes between me and my Calvins. - Calvin Klein Jeans
- I'd walk a mile for a camel. - Camel
- What's in your wallet? - Capital One
- For virtually spotless dishes. - Cascade
- Please don't squeeze the Charmin. - Charmin
- Get your own box. - Cheez-It

- Like a rock. - Chevy Trucks
- It's not nice to fool Mother Nature. - Chiffon Margarine
- Will you be ready? - Cialis
- Empowering the Internet generation. - Cisco Systems
- Live richly. - Citi
- "If I've only one life, let me live it as a blonde." - Clairol
- Does she or doesn't she? - Clairol
- The antidote for civilization. - ClubMed
- The most trusted name in news. - CNN
- Coca-Cola refreshes you best. - Coca-Cola
- The pause that refreshes. - Coca-Cola
- Have a coke and smile. - Coca-Cola
- "If you want to capture someone's attention, whisper." - Coty Perfume
- "Healthy, beautiful smiles for life." - Crest
- "Look, Ma, no cavities!" - Crest
- Cooks who know trust Crisco. - Crisco Vegetable Shortening
- Love it for life. - Dannon Yogurt
- A diamond is forever. - DeBeers
- You'll love the way we fly. - Delta Airlines
- We love to fly and it shows. - Delta Airlines
- We're cooking now. - Denny's
- Restoring the joy of motion. - DePuy Orthopedics
- We move the world. - DHL

- Yellow. The new Brown. - DHL
- Competition. Bad for them. Great for you. - DHL
- Aren't you glad you use Dial? Don't you wish everybody did? - Dial Soap
- The happiest place on earth. - Disneyland
- Time to make the doughnuts. - Dunkin Donuts
- The miracles of science. - DuPont
- Better living through chemistry. - DuPont
- The power of all of us. - eBay
- The world's online marketplace. - eBay
- "When EF Hutton talks, people listen." - EF Hutton
- Nothing sucks like an Electrolux. - Electrolux
- When you're crazy for chicken. - El Pollo Loco
- "It keeps going, and going, and going ..." - Energizer Batteries
- See your way forward. - Epiphany
- Quality in everything we do. - Ernst & Young
- Put a tiger in your tank. - Esso (Exxon)
- Don't just travel. Travel right. - Expedia.com
- Good taste is easy to recognize. - Fancy Feast
- Our business is the American dream. - FannieMae
- "Relax, it's FedEx." - FedEx
- The world on time. - FedEx
- "When it absolutely, positively has to be there overnight." - FedEx
- Play. Laugh. Grow. - Fisher-Price

- It's not just for breakfast anymore. - Florida Orange Juice Growers Association
- Built for the road ahead. - Ford
- Ford has a better idea. - Ford
- Quality is job one. - Ford
- Fosters – Australian for beer. - Fosters Australian Beer
- Fair and balanced. - Fox News
- Extinct is forever. - Friends of the Animals
- Say it with flowers. - FTD
- Imagination at work. - General Electric
- We bring good things to life. - General Electric
- Celebrate the moments of your life. - General Foods
- Two words to the wise. - Georgia Federal
- Babies are our business. - Gerber
- Shouldn't your baby be a Gerber baby? - Gerber
- "Look sharp, feel sharp." - Gillette
- The best a man can get. - Gillette
- Never let 'em see you sweat. - Gillette Dry idea
- Don't get mad. Get GLAD. - GLAD
- The best tires in the world have Goodyear written all over them. - Goodyear
- Leave the driving to us. - Greyhound
- It's a great time to be alive. - Guidant
- "Don't be vague, ask for Haig." - Haig Scotch Whiskey
- When you care enough to send the very best. - Hallmark
- American by birth. Rebel by choice. - Harley Davidson

- We answer to a higher authority. - Hebrew National
- Hertz puts you in the driver's seat. - Hertz
- 57 varieties - H.J. Heinz
- Invent. - Hewlett Packard
- Pleasing people the world over. - Holiday Inn
- The power of dreams. - Honda
- We're behind you every step of the way. - Huggies
- "Manly yes, but I like it, too." - Irish Spring Soap
- "Pure clean, pure Ivory." - Ivory Soap
- 99.44% pure. - Ivory Soap
- Don't dream it. Drive it. - Jaguar
- America's most famous dessert. - Jell-O
- Nothing runs like a Deere. - John Deere
- The right relationship is everything. - JPMorgan Chase Bank
- 100% juice for 100% kids. - Juicy Juice
- Every kiss begins with Kay. - Kay Jewelers
- Start aging smart. - Kellogg's Smart Start
- Finger-lickin' good! - Kentucky Fried Chicken
- Nobody does chicken like KFC. - KFC
- Kid tested. Mother approved. - Kix Cereal
- Share moments. Share life. - Kodak
- "What happens here, stays here." - Las Vegas Convention and Visitors Authority
- Betcha can't eat just one. - Lay's Potato Chips
- "When banks compete, you win." - LendingTree

- The relentless pursuit of perfection. - Lexus
- "Always a bridesmaid, but never a bride." - Listerine
- Because I'm worth it. - L'Oréal
- Magically delicious. - Lucky Charms
- "Melts in your mouth, not in your hands." - M&Ms
- There are some things that money can't buy. For everything else there's MasterCard. - MasterCard
- Good to the last drop. - Maxwell House
- Our repairmen are the loneliest guys in town. - Maytag Appliances
- Passion for the road. - Mazda
- Tastes so good cats ask for it by name. - Meow Mix
- Because so much is riding on your tires. - Michelin
- Lose the carbs. Not the taste. - Michelob Ultra
- Your potential. Our passion. - Microsoft
- Where do you want to go today? - Microsoft
- The champagne of bottled beer. - Miller High Life
- Everything you always wanted in a beer. And less. - Miller Lite
- "Tastes great, less filling." - Miller Lite
- Wake up and drive. - Mitsubishi Motors
- "When it rains, it pours." - Morton Salt
- Medicine with muscle. - Motrin
- Pork. The other white meat. - National Pork Board
- Must see TV. - NBC
- Break out of the ordinary. - Nestles Butterfinger

- All the news that's fit to print. - The New York Times
- Just do it. - Nike
- At the heart of the image. - Nikon
- Only fit for a king. Nine Lives. - Nine Lives Cat Food
- Enjoy the ride. - Nissan
- Connecting people. - Nokia
- Take it all off. - Noxzema
- The nighttime sniffling sneezing coughing aching stuffy head fever so you can rest medicine. - NyQuil
- Taking care of business. - Office Depot
- It's not your father's Oldsmobile anymore. - Oldsmobile
- The mark of a man. - Old Spice
- Grab the Southwest by the bottle. - Pace Picante Sauce
- The flavor says butter. - Parkay Margarine
- We will sell no wine before its time. - Paul Masson
- The taste of a new generation. - Pepsi
- "Pepsi, for those who think young." - Pepsi
- It takes a tough man to make a tender chicken. - Perdue Chicken
- Where the pets go. - Petco
- The best kept automotive secret in America. - Peugeot
- Famously fresh. - Planter's Peanuts
- Lifts and separates. - Playtex Cross-Your-Heart Bra
- The fun develops instantly. - Polaroid

- Get a piece of the rock. - Prudential
- Something to smile about. - Quaker Oatmeal
- RAID kills bugs dead. - RAID
- I liked it so much I bought the company. - Remington
- How do you spell relief? R-O-L-A-I-D-S. - Rolaids
- Get out there. - Royal Caribbean Cruise Lines
- Ingredients for life. - Safeway
- Experience success. - Salesforce.com
- Everything you love about coffee. - Sanka
- The beer that made Milwaukee famous. - Schlitz
- Funny name. Serious sandwich. - Schlotzky's Deli
- "Strong enough for a man, but made for a woman." - Secret Deodorant
- The uncola. - 7-Up
- "For the person who has everything, we have everything else." - The Sharper Image
- Cover the earth. - Sherwin Williams
- Always there in a pinch. - Skoal
- We make the money the old-fashioned way. We earn it. - Smith Barney
- "With a name like Smucker's, it has to be good." - Smucker's
- Made from the best stuff on Earth. - Snapple
- You are now free to move about the country. - Southwest Airlines
- "Now, that's better." - SPRINT PCS

- Obey your thirst. - Sprite
- That was easy. - Staples
- "Sorry, Charlie. Starkist wants tuna that tastes good, not tuna with good taste." - Starkist Tuna
- Eat fresh. - Subway
- Better snacking. - Sunkist
- "If it's not SuperSoil, it's just plain old dirt." - SuperSoil
- There's no equal. - Sweet 'N Low
- Think outside the bun. - Taco Bell
- Expect more. Pay less. - Target
- "If it's gotta be clean, it's gotta be Tide." - Tide
- Takes a licking and keeps on ticking. - Timex
- Choose freedom. - Toshiba
- Invest with confidence. - T. Rowe Price
- Get the feeling. - Toyota
- It's hospital recommended. - Tylenol
- The mind is a terrible thing to waste. - United Negro College Fund
- What can Brown do for you? - UPS
- Some of our best men are women. - U.S. Army
- Friends don't let friends drive drunk. - U.S. Dept. of Transportation
- "The few, the proud, the Marines." - U.S. Marines
- It's not a job. It's an adventure. - U.S. Navy
- The toughest job you'll ever love. - U.S. Peace Corps

- We never stop working for you. - Verizon Wireless
- Can you hear me now? ... Good! - Verizon Wireless
- Virginia is for lovers. - The Virginia Tourism Commission
- It's everywhere you want to be. - VISA
- Visine gets the red out. - Visine
- Always low prices. Always. - Wal-Mart
- Where's the beef? - Wendy's
- The breakfast of champions. - Wheaties
- Ring around the collar. - Wisk Laundry Detergent
- We're moving beyond documents. - Xerox
- Let your fingers do the walking. - Yellow Pages
- Ace is the place with the helpful hardware man. - Ace Hardware
- Plop plop, fizz fizz, oh what a relief it is. - Alka-Seltzer
- For all you do, this Bud's for you. - Budweiser
- When you say Budweiser, you've said it all. - Budweiser
- Have it your way. - Burger King
- It's the real thing. - Coca-Cola
- Things go better with Coke. - Coca-Cola
- We've got a taste for you. - Coca-Cola
- Just for the fun of it, Diet Coke. - Diet Coke
- Just for the taste of it, Diet Coke. - Diet Coke
- The best part of waking up is Folger's in your cup. - Folger's Coffee

- From the land of sky-blue waters. - Hamm's Beer
- Jell-O makes me mellow and the wiggle makes me giggle. - Jell-O
- Give me a break! Give me a break! - Kit-Kat Bar
- And America spells cheese ... K-R-A-F-T. - Kraft
- Maybe she's born with it. Maybe it's Maybelline. - Maybelline
- I'm lovin' it. - McDonald's
- You deserve a break today. - McDonald's
- Two all-beef patties, special sauce, lettuce, cheese, pickles, onions on a sesame seed bun. - McDonald's
- We love to see you smile. - McDonald's
- If you've got the time, we've got the beer. - Miller Beer
- Mr. Clean will clean your whole house and everything that's in it. - Mr. Clean
- N-E-S-T-L-E-S, Nestles makes the very best ... chocolate. - Nestles
- Pepsi hits the spot. - Pepsi
- You'll wonder where the yellow went when you brush your teeth with Pepsodent. - Pepsodent
- Sometimes you feel like a nut, sometimes you don't. - Peter Paul Mounds / Almond Joy
- Nothin' says lovin' like somethin' from the oven. - Pillsbury
- Away go troubles down the drain. - Roto-Rooter
- When you're out of Schlitz, you're out of beer. - Schlitz Beer

- Like a good neighbor, State Farm is there. - State Farm
- How do you feed a hungry man? - Swanson Hungry-Man
- I love what you do for me ... Toyota. - Toyota
- Fly the friendly skies (of United). - United Airlines
- Be all that you can be. - U.S. Army
- You're not fully clean until you're Zestfully clean. - Zest Soap

IF THIS BOOK HAS BEEN HELPFUL

Thank you for taking the time to read "Retail Shock Therapy". If you enjoyed it, please consider posting a short review on Amazon and also tell your friends. Word of mouth is an author's best friend and much appreciated! Thanks! Arlene

Stay in touch with me via:
Facebook: www.Facebook.com/fromideatoreality
Twitter: http://twitter.com/IdeaAndReality
For more information, you can visit my website at www.arlenebattishill.com
You can email me at arlene@arlenebattishill.com
Don't forget your FREE gifts at http://www.arlene battishill.com/bonuses!